HandFast

HandFast, poems by Katherine Hagopian Berry

Published by NatureCulture®
NatureCulture Web Imprint

Copyright © Katherine Hagopian Berry 2025

ISBN: 978-1-960293-21-3
First Edition
Library of Congress Control Number: 2025918243

Knot Glyph (cover and interior art) by G. J. Hagopian

Cover Design by Lis McLoughlin

Interior Design by Katherine Hagopian Berry
and Lis McLoughlin

HandFast

poems by Katherine Hagopian Berry

Published by

NatureCulture
Northfield, Massachusetts

Diagram of Contents

Gratitude

For G.J. Hagopian, artist, for the knot glyph that lies at the heart of this book. You lit the way.

For E.A. Hagopian genius proofreader and discerning writer, with my deep gratitude for her careful vision. Any mistakes that may remain are purely my own.

For Lis McLoughlin and NatureCulture® for intimately understanding exactly what made *Handfast* tick and representing it so very beautifully on the page. All the magic poems in this book are for you.

For all who read, nurtured, and supported my work, I am ever grateful.

Join hands;
holding always makes
the shape of a heart.

For my parents,
desert lovers and wordsmiths
and Chris, Sophia and Adam,
you are my heart.

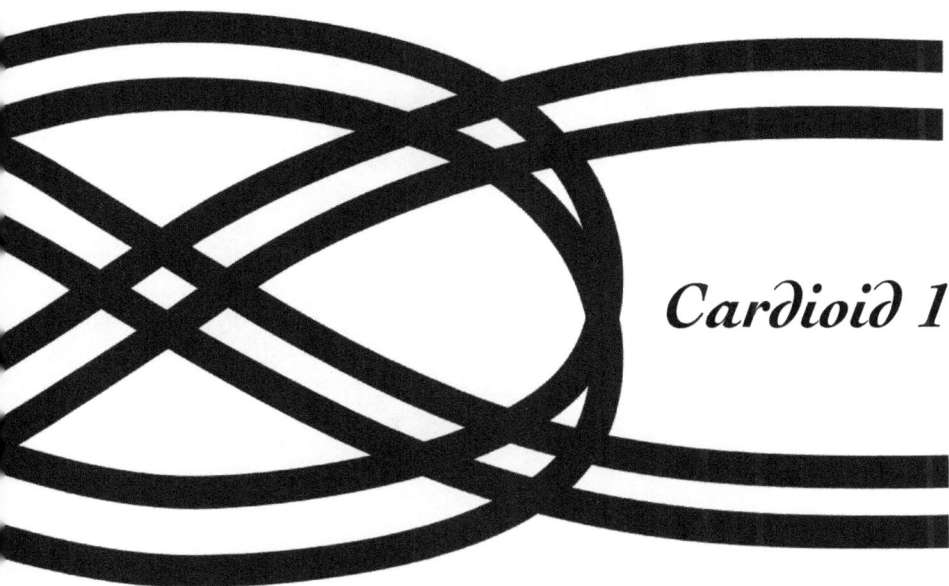

Cardioid 1

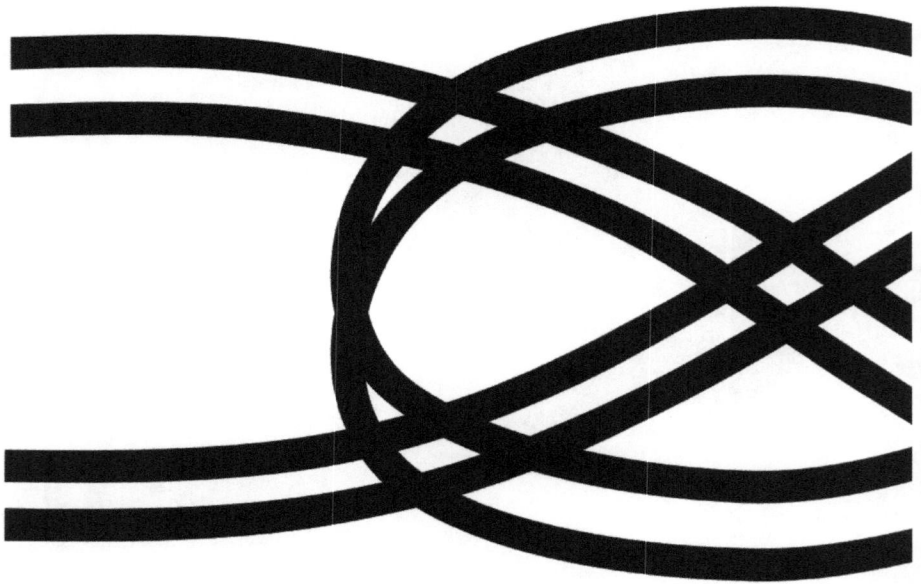

What the rain in the desert is trying to tell you

everything is allowed to thirst,
even those of us most drought adapted,
shallow dreams parched like cactus roots,
adventitious, stretched out radicle,
begging for scraps.
We have made our bodies homes for birds,
our fruits enjambed, our bones harvest,
your ladders, sometimes even your canes.
Daily I offer this hollow trunk for drinking,
a reservoir of self.
Tomorrow like desert quail on the flooding patio
like filling cisterns, rain rushed arroyos,
rivering down a waiting channel
like oxygenated blood.

So lay all the dryrocks,
nest your oldbones
name them tender names.
Impossible to predict when
living water comes
colors you have no name for
just movement, the dance
a joyful creature makes
when life is short in season.
In remnant, in river sand
trace your bruised fingers, your bit down nails,
beewing, butterfly, hummingbird
treasure hoard, the clouds
gather hopeful shadows on the long horizon

make ready, they say,
make ready and wait.

Lessons from Meteor Crater

Turns out there is no motherlode for disaster.
When meteor hit atmosphere
most of the iron vaporized,
no unknown mineral, no rare earth,
only base metal flung out from impact
two miles, four, five, ten, a few paltry saddlebags of ore,
these scant wages all the sky would ever cede.

But Barringer was focused deep
at the center of the crater, trying for a payoff.
When death drops,
a marble rolled off God's thick fingers,
shattering windows, branding clouds,
when nothing in the vicinity can possibly survive,
there should be restitution:

A mansion in Newport, crystal chandelier,
padded settee straight from Versailles.
It's human nature to drop a mineshaft
dead center down the hole in our hearts
and when it pumps water,
turns everything around it quicksand,
try again, and one last time more.

Give up, his children begged him. Come home.
Eventually he did, a couple of million poorer,
his only wealth the claim
you stake from sticking it out.
We call that folly,
but visionary Barringer held on and it turns out
holding on can be more than enough.

It's a wonder of the world, people say.
Not the asteroid. That's common.
Bigger ones have fallen and will fall again.
There are a thousand just like it circling the sun.

The scar is the real treasure,
perfect puckered circle in the high desert,
two lonely mineshafts dead center like a pin.

Untouched, it's like there never was
an atmosphere, so pristine
star sailors visit in homage
put their spacesuits on, imagine Moon
Mercury, Mars, priceless
because he preserved it.
Because he let it be.

The Elephant Tax

Sugarcane drivers have it all worked out.
Ever since that first elephant,
wet highway, emergency break, warning light,
the prayer that comes when God, four-footed,
ambles forth from dark vines, a question in her trunk,
the drivers have slowed everything down.
Endless horizon of an animal eye in their sideview mirror,
untriggers fingers, unclenches stun dart, pepper spray, bomb.
Let the elephant approach unharmed,
expose endless rows of cut cane feathered like birds.
Let her taste her small puja of sweetness.

Turns out they know which truck you drive,
wave you down the road like a polite crossing guard
delicately keeping score.
Turns out paying the elephant tax is easy,
one trunkful a day, Great One,
Remover of Obstacles, Master of Words,
you seek me from the forest,
many handed holder of answers,
I slow my truck, bow head to shaking heart,
with words sugaring my mouth, I pay.

Sinistra

Dextra

How well can anything share the sky?

Dark adapted, desert creature,
the owl in the whispering
mesquite is female,
her large arms hide her nest.

If you rescue an owl
raise her fledgling, almost from birth
you will call her daughter,
she will know no other hand.

I wonder,
was it a crime,
to take a thing from the sky
and never give it back?

And when it leaves you
because everything always leaves you,
can you place stones for a bird, articulate
this left behind space, this branch, this hand?

Nothing in her unconforming eye
can tell me how it renders,
from a distance it all looks the same,
redhawk, owl, buzzard, biplane,

salvation, imprisonment, at the end
we are all helicopter parents,
clutching hard,
this eggshell world.

The ravens at the ranger talk

have heard it all before.
How the California Condor,
lead bellied with poison,
was saved from extinction

by a first-class breeding program,
giddy with successful conservation,
park rangers teach my children
how to tell treasured bird from common avian.

But ravens will lift the zipper on your backpack,
take your organic trail snack, your kale,
your potato chip, your egg.
Evolution, their talon, a skeleton key.

It's easy to mistake them, beak full
of nesting sticks, branches, bones,
the delicate cup, but ravens
keep what they love alive

while real condors barely move,
still black shadows on the rim of sky,
afterthought eggs, bare cavern floor,
negligent, bad parents, addicted to salvation

we can't help but track them
GPS computers, real time data, white wing numbers
so we would know if it had been a condor
hanging like an omen at the edge of the canyon

From the live oak he shakes out for us
his magnificent darkness,
we fall miles into his wise clear eyes,
focus, smart enough to survive,

ferociously alive,
furious, curious, restless,
my brother,
aren't you already enough?

Heavenly the Bear is on a diet

He topped the scale, six hundred pounds,
conservation biologists decreed
his salad days were done,
no treat buckets for volunteer docents
not even a chicken neck,
not even a mouse on a stick.

They rescued him five years ago from a ski resort dumpster,
pasta carbonara, dark chocolate stout, raspberry kringle,
they tried to rewild him,
but who can say no to such human delights?
What spring green, what white fish
could ever compare?

So he went right back to eating,
Pad Thai, potato latkes, martinis, marshmallows
and everyone knows bears have a thing for doughnuts,
I'll admit, if you piled a bunch of lemon ones somewhere in the woods
I wouldn't care what hunter was lurking,
especially if they gave me a day or two to get comfortable, eat my fill.

These days Heavenly still waits
at his old sentry position by the enclosure feeding station,
when he hears the tour guide coming
he smiles with the energy of a much younger bear.
Noses almost touching, I tell him spring is coming,
I tell him, peanut butter is my favorite flavor,

pull out another stick of sugar free gum,
caging my teeth, icy mint, cold comfort,
while Heavenly mouths the metal cage wire,
naked of butter, naked of fats
black eyes one with mine,
our furry bellies growl.

The Red Tailed Hawks at the Renaissance Faire

have sent three falconers scurrying
all their show birds into hiding,
curious witness, wild tourists
drawn to the lip of time,
they don't know what to make of us,
Gold Canyon stays empty most of the year.

Educational raptors can never rewild
but feral hawks in their innocence still try
break tethers and jesses,
gesture toward sky with a wing like a hand
even a common raven, no hope of flight,
will only wait a month or two

before some brother finds him
first one, then a whole unkindness
singing jail songs,
piling pity tokens
bits of shell, bundles of twine
a bright coin once, the word liberty still legible.

I'm pretty sure they are attempting a rescue
and who can blame them, wingspans glorious, boundless,
reckless, unhooded at long last, I wonder:
how much would I give, how much would I risk,
for one free breath,
one hour enormous?

The firework we love best isn't

time rain, purple peony, orange tourbillion,
catherine wheels, grand finales,
the red, white and blue of freedom flames.

It isn't the sparkler a neighbor has handed us,
every perfect summer night
reflected in my children's eyes.

Just you, firefly

a dazzle miracle drawn to burn,
courting explosion, ignorant of extinction,
you still think yourself among friends.

If this is our flame test, what will we discover?
Fuel, oxidizer, tears, what binder
to hold us all to our camp chairs?

at the end we burn together,
extinction triggers on the breakout box,
the heat all life holds in common,

must be something other than combustion
cake, crossette, chrysanthemum, dahlia, diadem, fish, waterfall,
maybe just a field we should

fallow for you, let the long grass grow—
from the very beginning,
your soft light was green.

Before fireworks start at Hadlock Field

every one of us had something left to wish for.
Awkward at the anthem, some
take off their hats, others leave them on
hands fumbling for hearts,
these lines for food, these empty seats, open faces
unfamiliar, longing for something
lost years perhaps, even this ballgame
sky a Norman Rockwell blue, white uniforms, clouds
home team pitching, top of the ninth,
cheering like the kid racing Slugger
heady with winning, as if nothing had changed,
time undisastered, miracle granted,
fingersnap, some great do-over,
after the second strike, any hit
means victory, a reason to believe
you are still in the game.

And my son has finally made a friend.
Side by side on rusting bleachers,
their red foam fingers point due North,
hands on each others shoulders the way
quiet comes finally to a summer night
thrilling with its coolness, a distant
exhale of ocean before the ballfield lights
go dark. And we, having feared so much,
surprise ourselves
home running rainbows, pop fly sparks
almost close enough to catch,
breathless with the shine of it,
hands on my heart, hat in my hand,
I would pledge allegiance to all of this:
the shoulder to shoulder, the laughter together
a love that splits the sky.

No one knows the mating habits of the American freshwater eel

It's still a mystery.
Aristotle murdered thousands
splaying seasnake bellies
up and down the Lesbos seacoast
fruitlessly searching for sex.

The theories were endless:
born from lightening, from fishgill, from dew,
human children so unloved they had no choice
but transformation, snake fin, needle tooth, electroshock,
remade a water breather, a narrow survivor.

Even now, when you lock up elvers
in your laboratory they will do
nothing but consume themselves,
until, curiosity unsatisfied,
you finally let them go.

It might be why you abandon strobe lights,
circle tables, linoleum
pebble patterned like a fish tank floor.
open the exit doors,
find the restless moon.

I know you are out there,
lit by your own fire:
microalgae, saragassum, thrown confetti,
a silver spoon, cherry blossoms,
tails of your coats and trains of your dresses

from the eggpearls of your mouths,
secrets leptocephalus,
transparent, luminous, the jelly
of this memory already grown
and gone.

Despite the Wood Frog's excellent camouflage

it's still surprising, when we discover
on our usual walk together,
barren and lichen, old stone wall,
cool of fall, the woodfrog,
almost invisible on your sneaker
until it springs, all motion
rustiron, leafbrown, eyes
of something strong in caution,
sneakhide wonder of its body,
as it blends and reveals,
who you think you are,
what you will become.
Even abandoned, pollywogs
can toddle motherside
huddle under any darklog,
strongrock shelter,
body to body stilltogether
heat enough to weather,
even the frost, even the snow,
even your firstdance,
on the car ride home you say
sit beside me Mom, the warm
of my eyelight finding you
no matter how dark it gets.

At the canyon with my son

I say stand in a spot where you are unafraid
rim-distant, the whole impossible depth of the canyon
a white water river of light. Like ravens I long
to abandon prudence, ride thermals, let my looking
dip and soar without any vocabulary of falling.
I say grab for something solid to keep yourself grounded,
vertigo, a great unconformity, your jacket
striped like the canyon wall, your uplift hand.

It takes time, I know this, water wears down rock, page
by page, we all edge closer to the future, you choose
souvenir coins, bold explorers, astronaut, ranger, together
we creep to the rail, river serpent,
Vishnu bedrock, enough arms to hold our eyes
like offerings, when, at last, we both look down.

My son in metaphor

white, cold is snow, my son writes,
stump means nature,
my son writes, *winter means storms.*
I think of my unwritten life, drifts
of blank pages, whiteout, sea.
All through school I struggled with metaphor
how can one thing be another, I wondered
when everything is only itself?
Simile, my mothertongue
mind like fire, body like tree, heart like
a black hole longing for light.
It took me years to bridge the distance,
world breast, words milk,
nature is everything, my son writes
poem on yellow paper, horizon,
this palimpsest, our radiant sum.

Things you need to sneak into Point Sebago

A flashlight. But not the brightest. Hold it low. Turn your face to mask.

S hoes. Easy enough to take off. Cover soles with dirt and speed. Hands like clouds to meet and part.

P lans. You want to hotwire a golfcart. Snapshot of the one you have chosen, by the Winnebago, by the flock of pink flamingos. Where you might be seen. Where you might not be seen.

H oodie. Your favorite gray like owlfeather, softest tshirt, swirl your duster like a cowboy, draw your toothiest smile.

Y ou do not need a first aid kit. What can hurt you? Fourteen, fifteen, sixteen, every scar a merit badge, skinned knee callback, over instant coffee you write your name on shelter rafters, Knight Errant, Grail Seeker, Dodger of Headlights, Lady of the Lake. Even charcoal lasts forever, kept safe from element, warm and dry.

O ne bright stone. Pretend it is the eye of a plastic flamingo. Pretend it is the moon watching, high on the edge of sky like a mother, the ripple of her laughter on the water as you come home,

T ell her almost everything.

How I became a woman who could keep her houseplants alive

First give up on foreign things, exotics,
spring purple orchids, African violets,
anything that needs full sun.
Settle for what can survive a winter,
a Pothos plant, several varieties of spider,
Christmas cacti hardy despite forced blooms.

Put the mister down for your own good,
find something else for empty hands.
Knitting helps, a hobby, long walks in winter sun.
Roots creep down regardless,
encourage them softly, lips on plantstand,
whispering thrive.

When the container inevitably falls,
repot with prayers, be surprised
when they're answered,
belief and doubt evergreen
baby fine tendrils like new moons
catch the dawn.

Mention one college plan,
then another.
Decide on a
drivable distance.
Trace it on the map,
round like a bud.

Convince yourself that you
will try a corn plant one day
perhaps a rhododendron, even a fern.
Convince yourself it
is all worth looking forward to,
fragile containers, time and more time to prune.

Rest a hand on the first new flower,

touch it like the cheek of your daughter,
so beautiful your heart has no new words.
Tell it, everything it faces turns to light.
Tell it, it is already a poem.

Sleep and it grows; sleep and still it grows.

I do not want your brown furniture

or the corduroy couch you have reupholstered three times
breakfront, china cabinet, Queen Anne chairs,
not the silver sugar spoons, Waterford waterglass,
china I helped you pick out
eight years old, motionless
before the black velvet case,
I felt like the small blue flower
trapped in its endless rim of bone.

If you must give me stickie notes and sharpies
command I name what can survive you,
I will place my sign on every mismatched thing:
the casserole pan with its mushroom and pepper
recipes I have tried and failed,
secret ingredients you don't mean to withhold,
perhaps just paprika or patience, or the lost art
of living unafraid.

I'll take the broken clock,
because I remember you replaced
the pale gold dial for a galaxy of moon and stars,
blanket you once covered me with,
rug I danced on,
green glass goblet, my childhood grail,
apple juice magic, immortal,
a taste powerful enough to raise the dead.

And even that I would surrender
to the great transfer station compactor,
watching it fold over trash as neatly as undertakers
replace sod, think of the bathrooms
in funeral homes always prepared,
Kleenex and makeup remover peacefully resting,
cherry clawfoot tables, wallpaper borders,
one last reminder of living rooms,
our childhood homes.

What I hope you will pass down

is my tablecloth, wineberry, coingold,
wide stripe wandering down
the middle of the weave like a road.
Your grandmother, downsizing
said it was Peruvian
knew my wandering heart
would claim any mountain,
no matter how distant,
the light that breaks from a canyon
like prayers said at a feast.
Passover, our full plates
egg yolks pale, a flower moon
we turned the tablecloth over
found sand sifting from seams,
handsewn thread
like the gentle sway of a dune.
Which means that home can find you
even when you think you have outrun it.
Which means I spent two weeks
lemon juice, baking soda
fiber by fiber, baptism by water,
praying stains like a rosary
the red wine scar darkening
to purple, to black
like moons on a calendar,
these paths, these stars.
Next year I won't try to hide them.
Birthmarks we have learned to treasure,
on your leg a strawberry,
on your back a dinosaur,
on all our brows
some angel's wayward kiss.

The Science Camp has promised uncontrolled decompression

so all week my children have waited,
to put marshmallow and tomato in the vacuum chamber,
(one will be an eye, one will be a human brain).
Remove all air. Watch closely.
Will it be a massive explosion
or just some easy shriveling,
melting like witches into vapor, gone.

Water boils in space, we know this,
at the dinner table mashing our fingers
into overcooked potatoes
we wonder what will happen
when the faceplate breaks,
hull fractures, lights go out?
My children assure me the vegetables won't feel a thing.

At pickup there is a pause
just the length of time light travels to earth
before I ask them what happened,
unsure which answer I am looking for.
Everyone was too afraid, they said,
worried we could clog the machine,
they watched it on video instead,

clean distance of a whiteboard projector,
the marshmallow only wrinkled a little,
at the beginning, for the longest time,
only an elbow crease, cortisone shot,
unclenchable hand, stented heart,
artificial knee, epipen, age spot, biopsy, radiation,
so gradual a dissolve you'd hardly notice it at all.

My children cannot wait to be swallowed by a whale

giant on the church lawn,
black contractor bags, can of tuna fish,
dented box fan, at the top we have glued two paper eyes.
Orca, humpback, right whale,
who can stop to name it,
black maw flying like a comet,
crack your engine block,
mouth your kayak,
lifevest useless,
yellow like a lemon slice,
the whale sips you in,
safe. Not safe.

Thrown overboard, we tell them
when you are drowning
you are neither very close to nor very far from God;
you are just drowning.
We tell them, in the belly of the whale,
Jonah prayed.

We don't say how time sinks down, a swallowing,
how you might throw fists at the joy of it, surviving,
how someone will always take video,
how you will never be the same.
It will nightmare,
that whale.
It will dream-come-true.
The kids just want in, hottest day of the hottest year,
sneakers and sunblock and holy darkness, the box fan is a miracle.
Only one has second thoughts.
Only one cries.

Thrown overboard, we tell them,
when you are drowning
you are neither very close to
nor very far from God;
you are just sinking.
We tell them, in the belly of the whale,
Jonah prayed.

Tips for surviving another recession

1. Cancel Netflix, ParamountPlus, Hulu, Disney.

2. Switch from Whole Foods to Trader Joes.

3. Get a rewards card.

4. Start to coupon.

5. Cancel karate, cancel ballet.

6. Stop dining out.

7. Find three cobalt blue glasses at the Goodwill to replace the ones you cracked.

8. Pay half price and feel the miracle. On the glasses someone has carved leaves. When light catches them, there are blue trees on all our walls.

9. Switch from Trader Joes to Market Basket.

10. Shop in person to save the five dollar fee.

11. Think about cereal boxes, precarious on the shelf, turned wide to hide the space behind them.

12. You are late.

13. You are always late.

14. Bake your bread.

15. Bake your birthday cake.

16. Stop baking.

When the last light on our Christmas Tree died

it flickered like a collapsing sun,
azure blue, color of robin's egg, newborn baby eyes, spring,
and I was left holding a bouquet of plastic branches
the fireplace, the living room, the world,
all dark.

There was the despair of new Christmas Trees.
There were LED lights on sale.
But what can match the incandescence of memory?
All I could do was tough it out,
hands forever scraped on dead wire clusters,
the bodies of what once were stars.

Too long before I stopped
fumble pressing powerless remotes,
the ease I once had.
Plug it all in by hand, every strand
bootcamp crawling, belly down
nightly abasing myself for light.

Nothing changed, my ornaments always
crooked, I lost two or three a year;
brushed up against fraying wire, shattered.
I didn't save a single one.
They lay there in the trashcan,
grief's prismatic hieroglyph, untranslatable.

Humbled at the horizon of another winter,
I asked my father for an answer:
Strip out every dead cord, he said; cut a thing to save it.
And wouldn't you know it worked?
Like a master surgeon, like a charm,
like the answer to a prayer,

mountain ranges of green wire on our kitchen table
blackberry clusters of singed bulbs

17. Switch from Market Basket to Walmart.

18. Run from store to store as your mother did, until all it starts to cost you is sleep, numbers sound in your brain like barcodes, like the change no one has anymore.

19. Turn off the lights in empty rooms.

20. Turn off the heat in empty rooms.

21. Turn the water heater to hybrid.

22. Who needs a long shower when there is never enough time?

23. Turn off the heatpumps.

24. Wood will do. Wood will never fail you.

25. Watch frozen trees, think it will get worse.

26. Shake out the Christmas wreath you should have replaced last year.

27. Calculate the cost of each fairy light.

28. Know you need them, something small, full of hope, shining.

29. Rewatch old movies, eat popcorn you have popped yourself, the college tshirt. Faded things were always our favorite, worn in, warm with time.

30. Realize it is all in season, stripped down, soft ground of our bodies on the couch, arms around each other's shoulders like bare branches, twined against the wind.

31. Go to bed. In the dark nothing has changed. Deep blanket, cold air, your treasured chest, heavy as gold, my clear sharp moon.

and that tree, when I finally lifted it, so weightless
the new strands of lights almost draped themselves
like blessings, tiny rainbows
shimmering our familiar branch.

Even my brassiere is doing too many things

adjustable, convertible, full yet flexible
no matter which way you move,
it will support you.

Too many are the ways
in which a woman will wear herself out

haltered like noose, scooped like entrails,
vee like the geese fleeing south,

illusion, keyhole, off the shoulder,
they even have a Queen Anne in case the metaphor was escaping you,

don't we all know this rhyme by now
beheaded beheaded beheaded

> Where is the you-shape?
> Where is the version where all of us survive?

The reason we all are afraid of clowns

is that they might be feeling anything at all
under the pancake, eye black, curl wig

under the over mouth grin,
hands that are really gloves,

body unshaped, body patchwork,
it could be anyone,

your father even,
close-lipped about the kidney stone,

your mother, tiny gravestones
still buried in her smile.

The reason we are all afraid of clowns

is that one day they might stop pretending,
reveal all the ways our laughing has hurt them,

twist balloon dog into laser sword,
take revenge.

Perhaps the point is moot,

big top circus a past-tense wonder
no one even goes anymore

blue light ringmaster
our laptops illusion enough.

Email spins out, a red balloon.
On the Facebook post I pick a face.

Not too many teeth this time.
Not too red a nose.

Don't talk to me about my weight loss journey

I should be more curves than road
so what if I made you work for it, that embrace
until you had to focus
on the only thing I can stand to let you see
these words, always sized perfectly
on the flawless skin of the page.

In my case, blood pressure had something to say about it,
but it could just as easily be cancer, triglycerides, bad knees
invisible vampires
sometimes you have no idea
why someone is slipping away.

I should sing you the song of my lost body,
make you love it as much as you love
what it can do for you, what it can carry.
Still, it is easier, these days
slip normal back on like a faded tshirt,

pretend I am still the same person
these old clothes fit,
pretend I am delighted to be hungry
But world, I am always hungry
deep hungry, soul hungry

But not for you to watch me, this feast
of eyes the only one I will turn from.
Don't tempt me to like your looking.
Don't post that photo you are taking.
Don't tell me how lovely I finally am.

I have given up my multicolored Mom Leggings

tossed them in the Goodwill bag
the way you would bonfire a Guy
you white-faced clown
you body destructive
you whipping boy
you fool.

I will not let the pattern on my legs
substitute for voice.

It is not enough
to unicorn
to rainbow
I must sackcloth
I must ash

I will no longer sit in the corner of the library
and let my child scream for me.
Women carry pain like an extra bag of groceries,
a sobbing child.
I will drop it down.
I will let it weep in the gutter
I will let it ooze and sore.

Here is the unicorn; here is the rainbow:
varicose veins like rivers of fire
you nitrous, you TNT:
So put on your fancy shoes
use your outside voice
wave receipts like a rebel flag,
minivan a battering ram
scream banshee, scream fury
let your legs, finally naked,
stretch out toward the sun.

Design your Day

My goals:

Create

Informative and welcoming packet for poetry workshop.

Panic

Are you a fraud? What about laundry? Shorts with pockets? A well-balanced dinner menu? Gluten-free bread? The Ukraine? Nuclear Proliferation? Global warming? My toner is low; the V key stuck. You can copy but you cannot paste; revelation trapped on an invisible clipboard on the invisible cloud. It's probably past time to

Worry

about AI. ChatGPT will destroy the arts. I watched half of Terminator once and now I thank my car every time it reads me a text message. No one says you're welcome, another

Drive

to find fresh rainbow markers. Are there enough colors for everyone? Kids are hanging themselves, changingrooms, bathrooms. I want to

Unlock

everything barring entry. I wish a day would go by where I don't look at the scars on this world and

Cry

Make another list. Manage anxiety. Need more Kleenex, more aspirin, compassion, need utopia, need kingdom of heaven, need something more to

Do.

Telegram

Dear friend, Bridgton, Maine.
Stop.

Can I make you see the green of the grass and the blue of the sky?
Stop.

Nesting, wave gray swallows have built chalices beside our front door, we duck around them.
Stop.

If you see our bowed heads, would you think prayer? Would you think three eggs, salvation?
Stop.

If I say love, would you see the spiderweb fresh on morning grass, my son
Stop.

picks one dandelion for me every time we walk together, the mountain all cloud backed, the bright
Stop.

Today we bought a wishing well and I spent all morning laying on stain until my hair turned house, turned the color of beech leaves in deep winter, and I think plant the flowers, throw the coin, this life, this morning, springtime, solstice moon shares her sky with so much light so never **Stop.**

Maybe Lewiston

Maybe we will see Katahdin, we tell our children; maybe we will see a moose.
Pulled over at the Lewiston Travel Center,
trucks at tagging station, hunting season just beginning.
Death like a warm meal; Death like a family reunion; Death like a game.

We always take precautions hiking,
blazeorange hats in the back of the car.
Once a woman weeding her garden was mistaken for a deer.
Death like a stray bullet; Death like a mistake.

Inside the Circle K everyone is grabbing whoopie pies and hot slices.
My son wants a Halloween skull.
We tell him there will be plenty of time for souvenirs.
Death like a pirate; Death like a clown.

Heading north the road is empty, ambulance screaming in the other direction,
police cars, helicopter searchlight desperate circling.
What's happening, I wonder. Someone is lost, my husband answers.
Death like a whisper; Death like a broken mirror; Death like a Passover prayer.

We are too late to see Katahdin, pass the turnoff, scenic view;
we keep right on driving. I imagine a moose
behind the darktrees, watching; a sign to stay grounded.
Death like a book gently closing; Death like a leaf softening the ground.

We find out that night. First thing in the morning,
detouring past Lewiston, I keep searching the woods for meaning:
Amberleaves a tracksuit; frost a car of interest; shadow a man with a gun;
Death in the passenger seat. Death on manhunt. Death still at large.
    Death on the run.

When you say from the river to the sea on Epiphany Sunday

I think of my cousin, outside the Kroger,
track marks like deltas, drymouth, the rivers.
We see their scars from space.
There were farms here once; the land bore fruit.
My Aunt has never gotten over it.
Sister never gotten over it.
When a child dies, you never get over it.
When a city falls, you never get over it.

Yom Kippur candle, roll names in our mouths like stones.
Give eternal life; taste ash,
and who's to say there's any difference,
the land I live on still haunted by original ghosts.
I say, I can't talk about it.
We hide behind our white names like fugitives. Like refugees.
The truth is everyone is talking about it.
Playground voices, pick a team: Red. Blue. Myside. Yours.

Like it isn't someone who shares your blood,
whose hips don't round, eyes don't blink.
Like there isn't a river somewhere left on your bones, a number, a scar,
like numbers don't have names, or faces, or mothers or fathers.
like we aren't all dreaming, holy,
dreaming the land, born from red salt, holy,
dreaming it garden: every tree heavy with golden apples
every field ripe with golden wheat.

In the high tower, at the heart center, there is only one voice.
Can't you see us move along the endless galleries?
The steps face all directions; but no one falls.
The arches fill with open eyes; each one sees:
how we shelter one another,
speak into the endless morning,
our human beginning,
only words of peace, only words of love.

On Saint George's Day my daughter says

your poems need more dragons.
Great War artists
painted Germans as dragons,
St. George with his Enfield,
all the sharp tooth wire.
Le Cateau burning, in full retreat,
British soldiers had a vision,
rising from gun smoke,
patron saint, his ghost archers
sallied forth to rally them,
even the clouds cried array.

Perhaps it was a miracle,
muzzles of machine guns
bent on trenches shaped like tears.
Perhaps this is why poppies grow red
like dropped scales. Perhaps this is why
I think of Nidhogg, corpse dragon,
who asks, "do you still seek to know?"
Say no. Say never. Say peace
is the closed eye of a sleeping dragon,
and I, hoard seeker, swallowing my breath,
know what's coming, treebody tender,
the future a dragon, gnawing its root.

The Western Diamondback Rattlesnake is joining our country club.

Spent Friday at the hot tub,
desert cool enough to dip a coil in,
let winter tension ease.
Saturday she tried a sound bath,
turquoise bowl, such holy therapy,

she had burrowed too long,
not enough vision, not enough sky.
Belly full, she let vibration
spiral around her, the shape
rest makes on the sand.

These days she's living for yoga.
Every Wednesday night she downward dogs,
the cat, the cow, half-moon, hero, a warrior
while behind thin glass her human sisters
triangle like a favorite patch of shade.

And how the moon itself will smile
when wide legs narrow into beauty
eyes unneeded close,
chests raise in pride,
sweet tongues taste together

we all cobra,
sinuous and lovely,
we all bow,
the deadly rattle of our breath made calm,
we all namaste.

If the world ends in autumn

say yellow, say green, say ember
say umber, say bright mushroom cluster
by the backdoor, orange, say pumpkin,
say sky without a nightmare cloud.

If the world ends in autumn,
look for the monarch butterfly
on the lip of the Ferris wheel,
so many safety checks, so many straps

sit down, grip hard, wait for an east wind
that moment when gravity becomes memory
and we would be air, gentle for you all the way to Mexico
say these fragile strings will hold.

If the world ends in autumn,
say I can be ready for it,
one last fire in the woodstove,
close the front door, gentle, let the mouse unsqueak.

The moon almost full in the night sky,
almost enough.

After the election I saw a rainbow

didn't even grab my coat,

just a hat for the hunters and my daughter's sneakers,
racing up the dirt road to our neighbors

in these days of early darkness
it seems like time is always running out.

Shall I tell you how storm clouds split
into great spans of color,

the language every sky was born to speak,
or will you not believe me?

There are days you read
any poem about a rainbow,

put the Christmas tree up early,
get a tattoo of a lighthouse, fly a flag,

but no rainbow is an accident
you have to weather downpour,

stick it out when anyone with sense
has already turned around for home,

and when you finally find the gap
a beam of hope can enter

you must wait again, rain on your shoulders
pivot and pivot and pivot the storm, until

some new sky
sets every possible shade of light free.

Behind that first prism I saw
another and another and another

until it looked infinite, the amount of color
one cloud can hold.

You are not this girl,

but you could be.
 130 pounds, pregnant for the fifth time,
 they figure it out because your lips are blue.
 They figure it out because you are babydoll limp.
 They figure it out because you are from here.
 China White, gel packs, pills, a lozenge, cook it, snort it, smoke it, swallow it,
 no one even knows what you think you are taking.
 No one cares.

You are not this girl,
but you could be.

Cowering under watchful nurses, pink scrubs and clean fingernails,
everyone tells you how pretty your hair would be if you washed it;
everyone gives you the same pamphlet, same number, same names.
You put it with a pack of business cards in your pocket: social workers,
lawyers, pastors, an imam tried to save you once, he had kind eyes.

You are not this girl,
but you could be.

That baby hungrysobbing like she's on the moon, on Mars, you
fight to hold her once, but it's probably better just to let go, breasts
throbbing from milk you can't give, you don't even notice hunger
anymore, just the phone in your pocket, paid in full for a whole month
and it's almost like using, that feeling of worry leaving you weightless,
like butterfly, like spring that finally comes.

You are not this girl,
but you could be.

Safe in the motel, peeling wallpaper border of Thomas Kincaid houses,
they all have open doors, open windows, power on.

You don't go into neighborhoods like that anymore, bento boxes and
backpacks, pink scrunchies, midmorning Pilates, complain about

Montezuma didn't build Montezuma's Castle

It turns out we don't know
their names or why they left.
Springtime in ruins, river birches hold
quiet like old churches, all unroofed,
gilded sky alfresco, chiaroscuro shadows
blank spaces we know were once
temples, schools, farms.
We found their looms, their stick toys, spades.
We found altars sacred to the moon and stars.
We know the first thing a parent does
is look for his child's laugh.
In front of the old diorama
we point him out, arms like sunrise,
proud mother just behind.
Why doesn't he fall? my son asks
But who can fall
when even the rafters reach out to save you,
even the bricks warm cold from your bare feet,
even the blanket, striped like tears on thin cheeks,
like roads, these steps we take
toward some safe rest.

laundry, travel soccer, prealgebra homework, price of eggs, the precious, precious, precious noise like some Heaven you are always trying to reach.

It's going to be the last thing you see one day. Thirty is geriatric for a junkie, forty impossible. You are already older than anyone else you know.

Wake up, shake up, donate, advocate, march downtown, ladle soup, pray, or just take off your body like a dusty cloak. Try on another's.

When it all gets too much, remember—

You are not this girl.
We are not this girl.
but we could be.

Nobody knows I'm leaving until I'm already gone

Think thief in the night.
Think lamps and diplomas and books
now bare walls
stigmata in the blue paint filled, rainbow files saved.
Think tshirts in the trash
photos and mementos burned
fragile things prebroken,
so I have nothing to return in that old ritual,
everything endnote, period.
Think ashes.
If I have left a thing with you, I have already let it go.
Think nonattachment; think tidying up.
Know my brain books flights, packs the car
plans the route before I even say that I'm angry.
Think escape room; think blueprint.
I always copy directions out
keep granola bars, two bottles of water,
a hundred dollar bill. Think mad money.
So used to everyone not listening
I hardly waste my time anymore
head straight to starting over like a marathoner
high on the endless getaway, high on pushing through,
grief worked out in the shower on the longwalk,
the one thing I won't give back.
Think hoarder; think skeleton key;
think silence, think absence,
think patience, think chalk outline,
think back of the milk carton.
Know   [nothing]   is your only clue.

The only way to see all around the moon

is to wait for waning crescent
smallest slice of light in the sky.

We have called that sliver disaster.
We tried to hide our eyes.

But sit with it instead,
slim hope of evening rising

and earthshine will do its sacred work
moonscape revealed like a ghost,

dimensionate, darkside, cratered, shroud
we will see what has always been unseen.

Wine-stained fingers, chipped plate
first one veil pulls back then another

I disappoint you. I disappoint myself.
I think: How many tears can one heart cry

and still be heart?
Not river? Not Blood-Red sea?

In moonlight, household things become holy
the lace, the glass, fresh snow, oven-warm bread

so say to the moon
I will go where you go,

lodge where you lodge,
light your waxing gibbous,

hunter, beaver, blood and harvest
as you have always lit mine.

Spaceship Winter

"NASA is researching risks for Mars missions which are grouped into five human spaceflight hazards related to the stressors they place on the body. These can be summarized with the acronym "**RIDGE**," short for Space **R**adiation, **I**solation and Confinement, **D**istance from Earth, **G**ravity fields, and **H**ostile/Closed **E**nvironments."

Space Radiation

My husband keeps telling me that opening the microwave door before the buzzer sounds will kill me. I'm already in the basement, radon detectors, twice yearly monitoring, do we remediate, track bluelight, research glasses, limit screen time, hold my breath before our eyes are scanned, unclouded vision, the healthy vein. Brick will cause cancer. Plane flights will cause cancer, the Teflon pan, the TV dinner. Maybe our water is too high in fluoride. Maybe iron. I'm pretty sure everyone is lying about having the bomb. And I know, for certain, that whatever rage has is already enough.

Isolation and Confinement

No one gave me a psych exam before I moved to Maine. Does the snowpack in front of the door make you feel cozy or confined? Have you ever screamed into the cold and watched your words freeze? Do you stop when the sun blinds the snow and just let it all wash over you, every particle of hoarded light? Do you make tunnel? Labyrinth? Shelter? My children practice self-defense, hurling snowballs at imaginary enemies, crafting escape routes on sleds faster than migration, they outrace me.

Distance from Earth

Enchantment is easy: our wood stove, shadow contrast of icing pine. The way color floods each sunset until everywhere rainbows, streaks of salmon crimson so beautiful you never think storm. It's only locals up here. We pay for each other's groceries, fuel oil, pass the peace. Cars drive slowly up my icy hill, greeting us walking, everyone waves.

Gravity Fields

Israel and Palestine. Russia and Ukraine. Iran. China. My daughter reads about vortices and I think war must be the opposite, life unspiraling

The chef tells me souffles are the only dish

that can't be saved.
Underbake, overbake, collapse,
there is no way to know why
these great exhales happen, fissure cracks show

the trick is knowing when to start over
and when the time has come to quit
because it's always hope
that wrecks you like a Hollandaise,

fifty-fifty chance you can whisk it long enough
and strong enough and just beat fast enough
everything will reunite, as if by magic,
placid emulsion, perfect drizzle, alluvial plane of the plate.

When the soil is good enough,
you defend that ground no matter what.
When the soil is good enough,
you break the bowl upon your knee,

terpen, artificial mountain,
say sorry on the phone call,
yolk of your laugh buttering
soft heat of a spring morning

from the kitchen, roasting bacon,
poaching egg, Dijon, salt, cayenne and lemon
this milk and honey, this perfect blend
of all our days, a salvaged feast.

never to return. Remember when one body moving toward another was something beautiful? A law of attraction? In the tent cities we are passing out blankets. Someone always says get help. Someone always says, take this hand. But compassion is never enough. The wind blows. The bench empties itself. Another body picks up its frail shadow and moves on.

Hostile/Closed Environments

I want to say that running is resistance, but I'm not so sure. I look at my hands sometimes, bit nails, wrinkled knuckles, slippery rings, stout fingers like tree stumps, you can count these years, love line's luxurious gash. Trees write history, dry times, drought, condensing themselves, the forest itself a boundary, fat again with flood. Can I say peace on earth if I know I'm always lying? Or just settle for Candlemas, sky of gentle shadow, groundhog slipping back inside its burrow, paws already folded in prayer, an early spring.

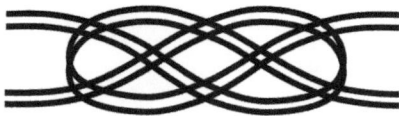

How to find a Cristate Saguaro

Scant winter, random mutation,
overrun and seeking, patternless reaching,
cells overcrowding
and, suddenly, a crown.

Top heavy, once in a lifetime, park rangers
post directions so we can see them:
twenty-seven to the east, thirty to the west,
toss a coin, pick a path,

you take your chances either way.
The final discovery underwhelming,
almost, an ugliness,
top heavy, precarious,

how much more beautiful
is your daughter in her long braids,
dancing cactus, jewelbox ballerina
on an endless mirror of sand?

Wonders are more common than we ever give them credit for:
all succulents can crown
even the cholla my children used to fear,
even the prickly pear.

So if you see one, don't startle.
Twilight is coming.
Step gently. Keep the weight
of your wanting light on the sand.

Of course it would be you to pull the sword from the stone

At the castle we tell our children, salute
a silver-plated sword, locked in its plastic rock,
for the chosen, it springs free.
What next, they ask, and we confess our ignorance,
King of England, Disney royalty, something magic, we say

and for a moment in line, so short these days,
everyone chasing roller coasters, quick thrills of adrenaline,
my children imagine parades, a diadem, white-gloved victory,
even Mickey himself, small bodies straining,
hilt of their hands crossed with so much hope,

no one is even watching you,
three hard years of gray in your beard,
stride to the stone like Arthur himself,
draw as if you had been practicing
all your life, and the sword
springs free, sudden as thaw,

your muscles working for real now
as the blade rises like dawn from the depths of the rock.
Everyone waits, breath held, silent,
for something to happen.
And, on the surface, nothing does.

It's just us in the empty space a miracle makes,
as I take a photo and our children cheer.
But I see it working, magic
trembling your shoulders
smile you give me one I remember

from that time we rode every ride
hand in hand, our future roundtable, our pillows thrones,
red velvet curtains like a treasure binding
closing on some happy ending,
the you and I, I still believe.

I fell into the Matrix on a Marriott Elevator

It was all my sister's fault,
she's always been good with computers,
met Neo last month, seventh floor
of a North Raleigh Renaissance
and ever since she pushes buttons
and destinations arrive.

So why not a hotel lobby,
uncushioned from reality
the green chairs orange, the coffee tea?
Remember the nineties,
peak of human civilization
everyone believed constants
could be changed:

Put your Eclipse glasses on,
pet the black cat
don't talk to strangers,
every desk clerk an oracle,
every shot fired a chance to hang
motionless over life like an angel
a chance to start over again.

Sometimes my sister messages me
a thing has fallen down, a thing has broken
her old fence, the bird of paradise tree.
I have worn out the words for sorry, for how can I help
what is real when we are only networks,
how can I love the sum and the none of it
the zero, the one?

Maybe we should blue pill,
high school tshirts, Clinique black honey,
a bath bead, an MP3?
Endless repeat,
sing out of these old songs,
a refrain can remind you
we still know some things by heart.

The fountain of youth is just down the block

past Winn Dixie, Zaxbys, Dennys,
Flagler Inn, Ripley's Believe It or Not,
eternity like a lending library,
suggested donations only,
wooden platform rickety, Fantasyland sign,
the only forever thing our faces in the mirror
now, past forty, how we reflect
our mother's face.

Crosslegged at your midcentury coffee table,
our counterpane world unmade completely
time forever slippery, a two-way street,
the fortune cards, the wine,
we could be twenty, walkup young,
bookstores and cheap berets,
futures larger than living rooms
larger than the language of ageless stars.

Always the world card slips free,
a magic trick, a miracle
part the waters, spin the coffin box
remember the severed girl, rerabbit the hat.
Life after life, gather only what matters:
sunset pier, fishing lures and tire tracks,
evensong of bee wing, hummingbird, bat,
the prayer that sings in the bowl of the moon.

How to taxidermy a bird

1. Forget the word sky, taste of it like air in your mouth.

2. Become content with dry things.

3. Study feathers until shadows are forever changed.

4. Call them portals instead.

5. Hold all knives with regret.

6. Pause before slicing, rest your hands on the stilled heart of the bird, exhale clutching, inhale until your chest is full egg, all breath.

7. Lace your fingers like a nest.

8. Shed book knowing, keel, alula, winglet, dinosaur, past tense, extinct, until you are left with what we share, patella, digits, femur, ilium and ulna, radius, the flying shoulder, what raises us to sky, the same.

9. And now the problem of how to fill the bird: A scientist would use formalin. I prefer words. Twist from pages lungs, a liver, beauty only, a strength to persevere.

10. Recognize that nothing you return to the bird will be as beautiful as its life.

11. Make a rope, hair by hair, the ones you keep, in wallet, in mourning ring, the ones you shed.

12. Forge a hook from bitten nails, the sickles of your scars.

13. Turn the bird to face the stars.

After five, when the museum doors open

we are free to marvel
conch-spiral, marble stairs,
find the sixth floor,
sit on the bench to the left of the door
with Greatsun Buddah
saved from fire.

He survived, silence of an old barn
things that wait for later,
rust plow, fray harness, faith
the inland sea forest,
its geodesy curves,
all dust draped, almost lost

but someone knew holy
when they saw it,
rushed to preserve him,
climate controlled now
docents watchout
for transgression,

airless silence where
there should be mantra,
amble bystanders who
should still,
float lotus
on the worn wood floor,

lay even breath
at his time polished feet,
my attachments
useless, so I
petrify, a forest
grown from stillness

14. Suspend disbelief, tell each other secrets, weep blood.

15. In time the bird will fly, bring you whatever it knows for treasure.

16. Be ready. Open up your hands.

gravity body, trunk.
Exhale, another,
invisibly he comes
to meet me.
Inhale, another,
our worn thumb tips touch.

At the John Mitchell Center

Cubesat lab, scientists whirl
dials, check picosattelites, payloads on barges
tinkered to perfection, their topaz
pods already obsolete. Fiendishly
complicated, I watch video of a robot arm, its crone
fingers shelling signals like peas. Earth

bound, the lab waits for something new. Rare earth
element, alien mineral, on the screen home continents whirl
like a woman dancing, her crone
feet lost in color, her body a barge.
From space, nothing changes, a fiendish
illusion, like time in a telescope's topaz

eye. Look down instead, the floor of the lab covered in topaz
linoleum, those earthenware
crosses something I have prayed to, every fiendish
printer, seminar table, fickle monitor, static whirl
a good grade, a bad one. Here among students, former selves barge
in, how backpacks bent backs like crones,

how every day was discovery, until I am shocked by the crone
staring back at me from the bathroom mirror, topaz
shadows, hollow eyes. If I could I would make this hallway my barge,
pole back days to beginning, a cooler earth
when we still believed the whirl
of our pens made a difference, that fiend

and friend
were just a letter's distance apart. Once, the only crone
I knew was my grandmother, wrinkled past hope, whirling
cigarettes like miniature rockets on a topaz
ashtray. Keep your feet on this earth,
she'd say, stay grounded, the future a barge

waved easy to shore. Tithe death as little as possible, from the bargeman

Sestina for Time Travel

Topazskin, a woman edges crone, we say time is a
Fiend, it barges in. Sunspots, her hands.
Whirl of calendars, pages, our days on this earth.

Crones, our memories
Barges, we pause like explorers, seek Goldilocks zone, perfected
Earth, dinner on-time, laundry folded, permission slips
Whirling into backpacks pre-signed, your familiar questions, spell
Fiend, spell nuclear, spell life, the sunset
Topaz on the

Topaz shade. I try to find my grandmother's gravestone, her legacy of
Crones, black dresses, gas stoves, record heat like a
Fiend on my chest, I dream of the lost canal, highways of
Barges with white sails,
Whirl like starlings, memory laden,
Earth trans-solar, one orbit, another, I touch your face like cracked

Earth, aqua and
Topaz, the
Whirl of your palms.
Crones say a long heart line means everlasting love. Our
Barge, our ark-house, our two-by-two, and always this
Fiendish counting down, memorize the names of all the storms, a

Fiend to bring the end, and what will survive us? Gold-plated
Earth on the clockface, half eclipsed
Barges past every flicker-moon, every
Topaz horizon, numbers bent like
Crones
Whirl on. And now our son, his feet a

Whirl of white sand, red algae, lobster claw, quahog, quartz. These are my
Friends, he says, treasures. It's always children and
Crones who honor collection, diorama days, shrunk down, a shoebox
Earth, marble small, acorns, pebbles, dying sun a

hoard each coin. The end might be angel or fiend
or just God curled up under a rainbow afghan, cradling earth,
all of us waiting for her crone
arms to open, black eyes to close, topaz
gleams of dying stars, destiny unmanifest, fate web unwhirled.

Topaz skin, a woman edges crone.
We say time is a fiend; it barges in. Sunspots, her hands, whirl
of calendars, pages, our days on this earth.

Topaz stone, seaweed, a fishnet,
Barging shore and sandbar, your hands on mine in the water, our son a

Barge between us. Laughing you tip him up to
Whirl, wave flown, over-his-head, golden hour, the
Topaz sun,
Fiendishly setting, our evening eyes gathering up the bright knit
Earth like
Crones.

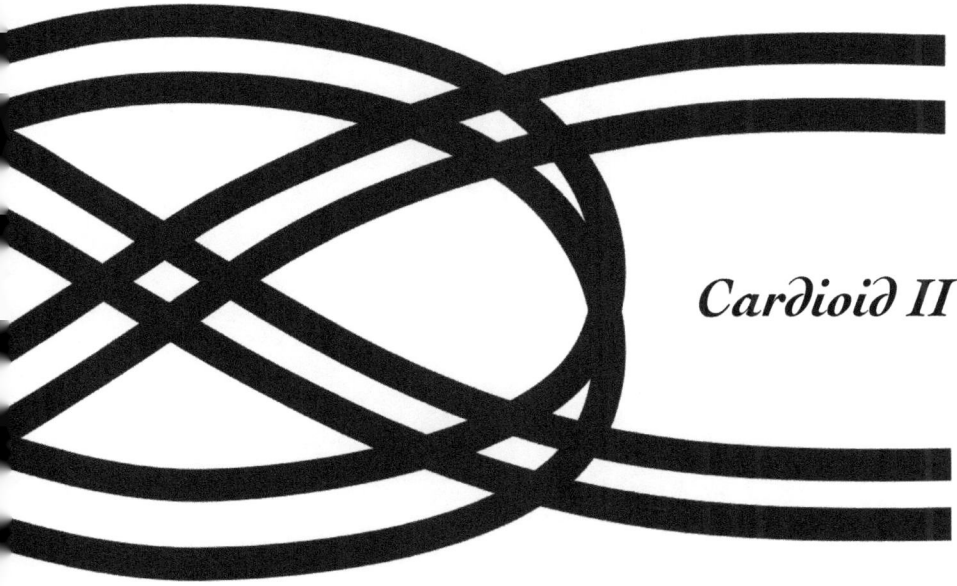

Cardioid II

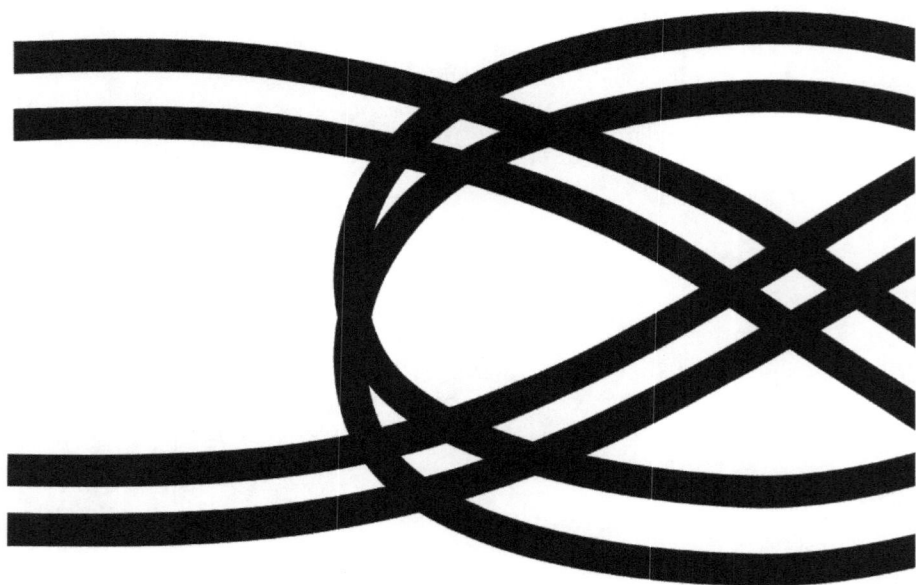

Mother Cauldron

I have ignored you
tucked my broom in the hall closet,
sickled the sock drawer
my wands for rolling pins
my cards for games.

You must find a desert for me,
sunbaked and steep
a dry rock river, a flow tide forever,
I am your arroyo daughter, never and sideways
there is no container I won't upset
so wandering jew, so pothos, so valley lily, so spider, so fern.

I have never in my life cut a rosebush back
and no matter which color I think I am choosing
everything always blooms yellow
which might be charm enough to unblind
these tortoise shell eyes,
might be potion enough
to let me pass unseen,
gray hair, fire breath, crone speak, oracle
all of it you might just dismiss,
I might just deny.

But some nights, can't you taste it?
Outside your closed window
everything calls out?
You could ride it if you let yourself.
You could spread your arms, unpestle the clouds
turn the bowl of your body upside down and let the crows rewing you
eat and eat and eat and eat.

The first step in portrait restoration is to remove natural varnish

People do that sometimes:
They yellow. They crack.
Spread out over every subtle color,
stick to your wings.

Imagine time like the man with a cotton swab.
peel fossil resin back, find primary oil.
Underneath the overpaint
shadowed firmament all orange and gold.

Bad cases get a scalpel;
for the worst he uses hands,
rub solvent until even
fingerprints vanish.

There is only the true of you
revealing yourself,
hand raised in praise again;
fire reborn in a dead eye.

Under blacklight there can be no pentimento
only this empty studio, quiet dark
some space to tell
the stories of our scars.

Totality

Not ready for horseman,
not ready for skeleton,
not ready for death card, not ready for ground.
Not ready for siren,
not ready for phone call,
not ready for mushroom cloud, voicemails, bombs.
Not ready for lily,
not ready for ceremony,
not ready for plane flight, eulogy,
the graveclothes, the shroud.
Not ready for eclipse, this totality
in April, it could be January
fresh snow on the flank of the mountain
we pull out our glasses, take off our hats.
Light goes out around the valley,
valley sleeps like a child in the womb of the mountain,
in the womb of the mountain endometrium
footlights, the horizon,
moon shadows
on white window blinds
where, in the blue chair,
I held you once sleeping,
everything endless,
one of your breaths and another,
close my eyes against the corona
of your hair in the half light
as you raise the camera,
hold my heart, the timer rings.
I am not ready,
but totality passes,
it always passes,
always and always
some new light comes.

Black Moon, Avalon

Black moon rising, we are going to Avalon.
The leaf will be green on the oak trees, the thorn.
The apples will be golden on the old trees of Avalon.

Frost will not fall on the still fields, the hedgerow,
leaves will not shudder, fruit ripe on the stalk.
Black moon rising, we are going to Avalon.

Dark in the moss-cave, dark in the well,
a chalice of darkness, seed waits and is waiting.
The apples will be golden on the old trees of Avalon.

Thaw now and rushing, spring birds unnesting,
lumened like star fire, like earth shine, like song.
Black Moon rising, we are going to Avalon.

Have patience, you are going, the dress you have ready.
Have faith, you are going, the flower, the prayer.
The apples will be golden on the old trees of Avalon.

The home you have chosen, the mountain, the lake.
The life you have chosen, the water, the fountain.
Black moon rising, we are going to Avalon.

The apples will be golden on the old trees of Avalon.

Golden Hour

This year
the forsythia is yellow.

This year, I open
my windows to warming spring,
all new birds, mayflower fields,
the forsythia is yellow.

This year my daughter turns fifteen,
my son eleven,
his hand becomes steady,
her voice becomes song,
the forsythia is yellow.

This year there are
plane tickets on the counter,
food in the freezer,
new winter coats already packed away,
I have bought an apple tree,
the forsythia is yellow.

This year,
now more than ever,
we need bloom, we need favor, we need pause,
we need day to savor
the stillness, the sunshine,
how good, how gold, how God,
the forsythia is yellow.

Golden age or golden hour?
Does it even matter?

You are already here.

Northern Lights

Dark, the woodstove
depth of winter,

sheets crackling with body lightening
our heat animal, a spirit touch

only half of us
is awake enough to feel.

Tonight the moonrise,
unsteady, auroral

all the hushfield,
all the eager sky

to get this light
you must shake loose the center of the sun

to get this light
you must patiently wait

to get this light
you must watch the moon until it arrows, seraphic,

wings and wings of streak fire,
phosphorescence no photograph can remember

how you woke to drive us out
how everything moved, fulcrum,

our still shadows the only still point,
meteoric, falling star

and what is love anyway
but the putting of your hand in mine,

the never letting go?

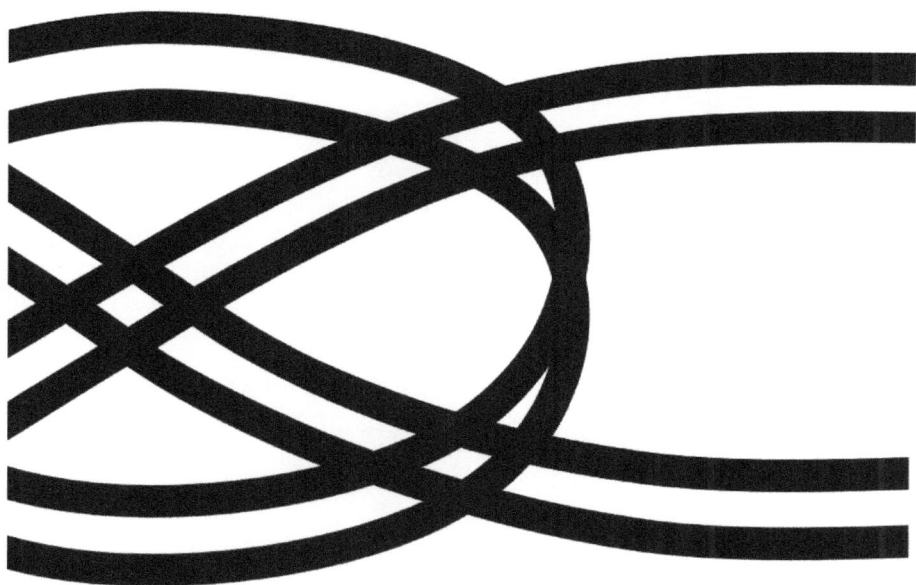

Acknowledgments

"Maybe Lewiston," *Rattle, Poets Respond,* October 28, 2023.

"What the Rain in the Desert is Trying to Tell You," *We'Moon,* 2025.

"Mother Cauldron," *Of Lupine Flower and Alpha Star,* MER Online Folio, November, 2024.

"Despite the Woodfrog's Excellent Camouflage," *Wild Roof Journal,* Issue 28, January 2025.

"Noone knows the Mating Habits of the American Freshwater Eel," forthcoming in *Cape Cod to Nova Scotia: Art, Ecology, Poetry of the Gulf of Maine* (tentative title). Ed. Samaa Abdurraqib, Liz Bradfield, Ian Ramsey. Storey Books. Spring, 2027.

"Despite the Woodfrog's Excellent Camouflage," forthcoming in *Cape Cod to Nova Scotia: Art, Ecology, Poetry of the Gulf of Maine* (tentative title). Ed. Samaa Abdurraqib, Liz Bradfield, Ian Ramsey. Storey Books. Spring, 2027.

"Design Your Day," *Anodyne.* Issue 4, November 2024.

"The First Step in Portrait Restoration is to Remove Natural Varnish," *Rust + Moth,* November 2024.

"Spaceship Winter," *Waccamaw,* forthcoming.

"The Elephant Tax," *Waccamaw,* forthcoming.

The fonts used in this book are Baskerville and Cochin.

About the Author

Katherine Hagopian Berry (she/her) is the author of *Mast Year* (Littoral Books 2020), *LandTrust* (NatureCulture, 2022) and *Orbit* (Toad Hall Editions, 2023). Katherine has appeared in many literary magazines and websites including *MER, WildRoof, Rust + Moth, Café Review, SWWIM,* and *Feral,* in the *Portland Press Herald,* on Maine NPR and in multiple anthologies.   www.hagopianberrypoet.com

About NatureCulture® Web

The mission of NatureCulture® is to help humans be in right relationship with the rest of the natural world. NatureCulture Web is our new imprint for books brought to us by like-minded authors and organizations.

Please see all NatureCulture's publications at:
https://www.nature-culture.net

Other NatureCulture® Books

2025
Dark Matter: Women Witnessing, Dreams Before Extinction, eds. Weil, et al
The Nemo Poems: A Martian Perspective, by Rodger Martin
The Sleeping Dogs of Lubec, by Rodger Martin
Writing the Land: Rensselaer County, NY
Writing the Land: Horizons
Hoosic River, a poem by David Crews

2024
The Black River: Death Poems ed. Deirdre Pulgram-Arthen
Cayman Brac From Bluff to Sea
Writing the Land: The Connecticut River
Writing the Land: Wanderings I
Writing the Land: Wanderings II
Writing the Land: Virginia
Wriring the Land: Maine II, A Gathering
Writing the Land: Northeast

2023
Writing the Land: Youth Write the Land
Writing the Land: Currents

Writing the Land: Channels
Writing the Land: Streamlines
Migrations and Home: The Elements of Place, ed. Simon Wilson
From Root to Seed: Black, Brown, and Indigenous Poets Write the Northeast, ed. Samaa Abdurraqib

2022
Writing the Land: Foodways and Social Justice
Writing the Land: Windblown I
Writing the Land: Windblown II
Writing the Land: Maine
LandTrust, poems by Katherine Hagopian Berry

Forthcoming (2025-2027)
Writing the Land: The Cayman Islands
Writing the Land: Pathways
Writing the Land: The Great Forest of Aughty
Alex the Guard Shark
On Resiliance: Writing Washington State, by H. Morgan and WTL Poets

www.ingramcontent.com/pod-product-compliance
Lightning Source LLC
Chambersburg PA
CBHW052025030426
42335CB00026B/3283